Little Pebble™

T0052272

Mammals in the Wild

Tigers

by Kathryn Clay

PEBBLE
a capstone imprint

Pebble Books are published by Pebble
1710 Roe Crest Drive, North Mankato,
Minnesota 56003
www.mycapstone.com

Copyright © 2019 by Pebble, a Capstone imprint. All rights reserved. No part of this publication may be reproduced in whole or in part, or stored in a retrieval system, or transmitted in any form or by any means, electronic, mechanical, photocopying, recording, or otherwise, without written permission of the publisher.

Library of Congress Cataloging-in-Publication Data
Names: Clay, Kathryn, author.
Title: Tigers : a 4D book / by Kathryn Clay.
Description: North Mankato, Minnesota : an imprint of Pebble, [2019] | Series: Little Pebble. Mammals in the wild | Audience: Age 4-7.
Identifiers: LCCN 2018004133 (print) | LCCN 2018009138 (ebook) | ISBN 9781977100887 (eBook PDF) | ISBN 9781977100764 (hardcover) | ISBN 9781977100825 (paperback)
Subjects: LCSH: Tiger—Juvenile literature.
Classification: LCC QL737.C23 (ebook) | LCC QL737.C23 C536 2019 (print) | DDC 599.756—dc23
LC record available at https://lccn.loc.gov/2018004133

Editorial Credits
Karen Aleo, editor; Juliette Peters, designer;
Tracy Cummins and Heather Mauldin, media researchers;
Laura Manthe, production specialist

Photo Credits
Getty Images: Picture by Tambako the Jaguar, 11;
Newscom: Theo Allofs/Minden Pictures, 17; Shutterstock: Dzmitry Kim, Design Element, George Lamson, 21, Nachiketa Bajaj, Cover, Natasha Zalevskaya Design Element, neelsky, 13, niall dunne, 19, Pablo77, 15, Richard Constantinoff, 7, Sarah Cheriton-Jones, 5, Tiago Jorge da Silva Estima, 1, Yvdalmia, 9

Printed in the United States 5559

Table of Contents

At Home 4

Big Cats 10

Baby Tigers 18

Glossary 22
Read More 23
Internet Sites 23
Critical Thinking Questions . . 24
Index 24

At Home

A big cat lies in the grass.

It's a tiger!

Tigers are mammals.

Mammals have hair or fur.

They have warm blood.

Tigers can be found in forests.

Others live in tall grass.

Big Cats

Tigers have big paws.

Their claws are sharp.

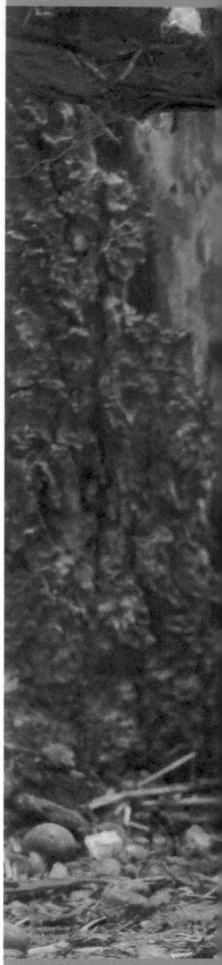

Tigers have orange fur.

They also have dark stripes.

Each stripe is different.

Tigers wait.

They hide behind bushes.

Tigers hunt.

Roar!

A tiger leaps.

It chases the prey.

Baby Tigers

Look!

Here are two cubs.

They start out small.

Cubs drink milk.

They grow up fast.

Glossary

claw—a hard curved nail on the foot of an animal

cub—a young tiger

forest—land filled with trees that grow close together

hunt—to find and catch animals for food

leap—to jump a long way

mammal—a warm-blooded animal that breathes air; mammals have hair or fur; female mammals feed milk to their young

paws—the feet of animals with four feet and claws

prey—an animal hunted by another animal for food

Read More

Archer, Claire. *Tigers. Big Cats.* Minneapolis: Abdo Kids, 2014.

Hall, Margaret. *Tigers and Their Cubs: A 4D Book.* Animal Offspring. North Mankato, Minn.: Capstone Press, 2018.

Statts, Leo. *Tigers.* Savanna Animals. Minneapolis: Abdo Zoom, 2017.

Internet Sites

Use FactHound to find Internet sites related to this book.

Visit www.facthound.com

Just type in 9781977100764 and go.

Check out projects, games and lots more at **www.capstonekids.com**

Critical Thinking Questions

1. Adult tigers catch prey. What does prey mean?
2. Where do tigers live?
3. What do cubs drink?

Index

cats, 4
claws, 10
cubs, 18, 20
forests, 8
fur, 6, 12
grass, 4, 8
hair, 6
hunting, 14
leaping, 16
mammals, 6
milk, 20
paws, 10
prey, 16
warm-blooded, 6